THE IDEA
GENERATOR

KEN HUDSON has worked in senior roles for over fifteen years in marketing, advertising and management consulting. He has worked with many leading brands including Heinz, Wrigley, Colgate, Kellogg's, Unilever, Disney, DuPont and Nestlé. He teaches Marketing Creativity at the University of Technology, Sydney.

Visit his website at **www.ideaspace.com.au**

THE IDEA GENERATOR

60 Tools for Business Growth

KEN HUDSON

Atlantic Books
London

First published in 2007 by Allen & Unwin,
83 Alexander Street, Crows Nest NSW 2065, Australia.

First published in Great Britain in 2008
by Atlantic Books, an imprint of Grove/Atlantic Ltd.

9 8 7 6 5 4 3 2 1

A CIP catalogue record for this book is available
from the British Library.

978 1 84354 762 4

Printed in Great Britain

Atlantic Books
An imprint of Grove Atlantic Ltd
Ormond House
26–27 Boswell Street
London
WC1N 3JZ

CONTENTS

To Margot—my partner in life

To Charlotte and Molly—my inspiration

To Bill, Margaret, Ray and Gloria—my mentors

This book is also dedicated to the friendship and sage
advice of another idea generator—Dr Paul Leinberger

INTRODUCTION

The business world is moving at an ever-increasing pace. Product life cycles are getting shorter and shorter. Consumers and retailers want better products, sooner. Shareholders demand higher performance and faster results. Employees expect a better work/life balance and want their bosses to act in a responsible and sustainable way.

But just as managers are facing these spiralling pressures they are being given fewer people, a smaller budget and, perhaps most importantly, less time. As a result, many managers and leaders feel stranded or 'stuck'. They know intuitively that what has worked in the past will no longer work in the future. Their business school education no longer equips them with the tools to address the realities of a changing marketplace.

The biggest challenge is to look at these issues from a fresh perspective. For example, by redefining the circus experience, the Canadian troupe Cirque du Soleil has been able to achieve great success. It was not bound by what a circus had been, but what it could be.

I call this process 'becoming unstuck'—moving beyond a rigid view to a more dynamic and productive one. Changing your mindset enables you to out-think and out-imagine your competition. And to achieve this goal you need a new set of tools.

Stuck	Unstuck
• Trapped by precedent	• Set free by imagination
• Incremental growth	• Non-linear growth
• Familiar ideas and solutions	• Breakthrough ideas and solutions
• Career blockage	• Unlimited opportunities

The Idea Generator provides practical, effective tools that will improve the productivity of your thinking. The tools in this book can be learned by anyone, at any level, regardless of role or education and have been tested over a number of years in hundreds of workshops.

The *Idea Generator* model

In most situations there are two elements: the problem (the challenge, goal or opportunity you are currently dealing with) and the way of 'seeing' this problem (your lens, mindset or perception).[1]

I have called the current problem 'P1' and the current lens in use 'L1'. If you always use the same problem or P1 and you view this problem with the same lens or L1, it should not surprise you when you obtain the same outcome.

For example, if your P1 is how to increase customer satisfaction, and you continue to look at this problem with the same L1—it is the responsibility of the customer service manager—then the outcome will probably not vary considerably from last year's results.

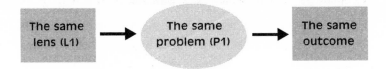

If you need a different and potentially better outcome, there are two key strategies.

1. Change the problem (what I call P2)

Let's continue with the previous example. If you change the problem to 'What would it take to make our customers feel more passionate about our business?' (P2), this immediately leads to different ideas, such as inviting customers to solve their own complaints or encouraging customers to visit the business and meet the staff.

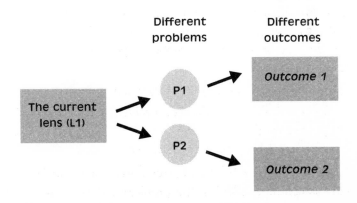

2. Change the lens (what I call L2)

Another key strategy is to look at the problem with a new lens (L2). For example, what if you looked at the previous problem from a purely financial point of view? You might decide that trying to improve customer satisfaction for every customer is uneconomic. From a financial perspective, it may be better to dramatically improve the service for your profitable customers and reduce service levels for the unprofitable customers.

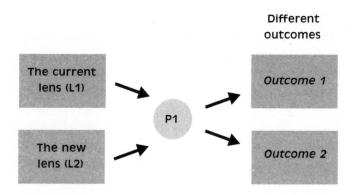

In both of these examples, the twin thinking strategies of either changing the problem and/or changing the lens have opened up an array of new ideas and possible solutions. My experience is that the process of shifting from P1 to P2 and/or L1 to L2 is one that can be learned by anyone using the range of tools outlined in this book.

Here is a real-life example of this approach. The leaders of a major garbage bag brand were struggling with how to grow their market share and improve profit margins. When I began working with them, their collective mindset (or L1) was that garbage bags were a 'low interest and low involvement' category (marketing speak for a category where consumer engagement is low, compared with mobile phones where interest is high). It defined the direction of all their marketing efforts, and consequently their emphasis on price promotions. My suggestion was that they needed to create a new way of seeing garbage bags. They tried the lens, 'garbage bags can be interesting', which enabled them to generate a number of breakthrough ideas. These led to the development of deodorising garbage bags, which have been launched with great success.

Then I challenged the leadership team to create a range of interesting new problems. They had, for instance, accepted as a given the consumer belief that putting out the garbage is messy and unpleasant. So they asked: 'How can we make garbage bags easier to use?' This resulted in the creation of a garbage bag on wheels, which is the next product to be tested. The leadership team is now brimming with new ideas and opportunities to grow their brand and business. The garbage bag itself has not changed. What has altered is their lens and how they redefined the problem of using a garbage bag.

The single lens error

These new ideas seem obvious only when you view garbage bags through a new lens. Why didn't the management team see these opportunities before? The answer lies in the nature of your mindset—the lens you use to perceive the world. Your mindset enables you to interpret and make sense of your environment but it also can limit your view to a narrow and well-explored range of possibilities[2] that are informed by your previous experiences, values, assumptions and beliefs.[3]

Information (e.g. a market trend) that is consistent with your mindset tends to be reinforced while other information (e.g. a competitive inroad) that is inconsistent with your mindset is often downplayed. This is why industry leaders find it so difficult to develop bold, innovative products. They are limited by the lens through which they see the world.

Consider, for example, a house being renovated. What do the various people involved in the project 'see'?

- The homeowner 'sees' a home.
- The builder 'sees' a steady income stream.
- The tradesman 'sees' a job.
- The neighbour 'sees' noise and disruption.

Which lens is correct? The answer is that all are correct and equally valid. But each lens only represents a partial view. Hence, the *Idea Generator* method involves shifting your current lens to obtain a more complete or different view of a situation.

The tools in this book will enable you to change your lens at will. This means new ideas and opportunities because the shift of view can be quite dramatic, much like the *Mona Lisa*, which reveals more of its character from different viewings. Consider the following comment from the former CEO of General Electric, Jack Welch:

> They [a future leaders team] said we needed to redefine our current markets so that no business would have more than 10 per cent market share. That would force everyone to think differently about their business. This was the ultimate mind-expanding exercise as well as market-expanding

breakthrough. For nearly 15 years, I had been hammering away the need to be number one or number two in every market. Now this team was telling me that one of my most fundamental ideas was holding us back. I told them I loved the idea.[4]

For another example, think about how business leaders are viewing their environmental footprint. In years gone by, 'being green' was seen only in terms of an increase in costs. Now, more and more leaders see the environment as a huge business opportunity. General Electric, through its Ecoimagination program to cut carbon emissions, has delivered over $10 billion in sales.[5]

Creating a new lens to see a situation more clearly can also be used in your personal life. My eldest daughter Charlotte loves horses, and I was determined to support her desire to learn how to ride. But I was very nervous when I approached my horse, which in turn made the horse difficult to control and further increased my reluctance to get on it. This stand-off was resolved when I created a new lens (L2)—'the horse was just like a big dog'. I love dogs and have always been very comfortable around them. This new lens led to an instant calm that enabled me to ride the horse and enjoy the experience.

The single problem error

The other barrier to innovative thinking is the belief there is only one way to define a problem. My experience is that continuously using the same problem (P1) narrows the range of possible solutions. Some P1s may be more appropriate than others but each can lead to a new, workable solution. For example, I recently facilitated a group that was trying to create new ideas to combat kids' obesity but our ideas were following a well-worn path. So I encouraged the group to develop a new way of defining the problem (a P2). They decided that a more fertile challenge was to consider ways of enhancing kids' health. This meant that the group could consider the problem in a more holistic, proactive way. They realised that weight was only a part of kids' health. What about their physical, emotional and even spiritual wellbeing? This new challenge led to a much broader and more original set of ideas, which have since been presented to many government agencies.

Another reason for the continued use of a single P1 is the belief that there is a single best answer. This might be so for mathematics but the real world does not function with the rigidity of numbers. In business, there are many different, interrelated factors to consider when making any decision and many ways of defining a problem. The nature of business changes day by day and what works today may not work tomorrow. By not challenging a P1 in a dynamic world you are bound to fail.

People in business are encouraged to be action-oriented, with rewards and recognition going to the people who are good at solving problems. This emphasis on problem-solving has many benefits but comes at a cost. By only focusing on solving problems, you can neglect the importance of creating more original questions. Spending more time on defining a fresh set of questions can unlock new solutions.

Becoming 'unstuck'

Together, the single lens error and the single problem error amount to a feeling for many managers of being 'stuck'. The significance of this feeling is profound. Having a limited array of options or ideas means that your performance suffers as pressure mounts. Your results tend to be slow and incremental. What's more, it creates a negative cycle where your expectations of yourself remain low. This in turn affects your performance and confirms your low expectations.

You need to interrupt this way of thinking. The biggest irony is that being 'stuck' is largely due to factors within your control.

Try this exercise:

> How many different uses can you think of for a mobile phone? Most people give between five to eight answers.
>
> Now try to answer this slightly different question (P2)— How many *unusual* uses can you think of for a mobile phone?
>
> Try a third way of looking at it. Imagine that you are an ant (L2). What possible uses can you think of for a mobile phone? You'll be surprised by the new possibilities you've just imagined.

The mobile phone is a metaphor for any problem, challenge or opportunity. Your responses to the initial problem are limited by your life experiences and assumptions. By redefining the problem (P2) and/or using a new lens (L2) you have created a rich array of new possibilities from which to choose a better outcome. Suddenly you have movement and a way forward.

The challenge for anyone in business who wants to gain an edge is to learn how to think and act more quickly than the competition. *The Idea Generator* provides a practical, tangible way for anyone in business (or life generally) to create a better, more fulfilling and productive future.

A note on the tools

The tools described in this book have all been tested and proven to be effective in many different businesses across a vast array of industries and circumstances. Some tools will be more appropriate for your situation than others; much will depend on your personal preferences. Understanding that it is within your power to find solutions and get ahead in business is the first and most important step. Use the tools in the following pages as a starting point to push you in the right direction.

The structure of *The Idea Generator*

Each chapter contains ten tools, which are described on the left-hand pages. Examples of how the tools can be applied are given on the right-hand pages. The tools are flexible and can be used in many different situations. Each chapter includes tools that follow the two key strategies of changing the lens and/or changing the problem definition.

How to get the most out of this book

There is no right or wrong way to use this book. You can start at the front and work through methodically. Or you can select a tool at random and apply it to the situation at hand. The aim is to try to master a number of tools to create different solutions. After reviewing each tool, ask yourself 'How can I apply this specific tool to my situation?' By answering this question, you can customise the tools to your brand, business or career.

THE IDEA
GENERATOR

'The real voyage of discovery consists not
in seeking new landscapes, but in having
new eyes.'

Marcel Proust

TEN TOOLS TO SOLVE PROBLEMS IN A MORE POWERFUL WAY

1

Think in threes

Business people often think in opposites: right/wrong, accept/reject, pass/fail, yes/no. This kind of thinking tends to restrict the possible number of solutions to a problem and make everything seem black and white.

But the world is not binary. High performers must think in a more expansive way. Effective human resource managers, for example, not only have to find innovative ways of attracting people to a business but also how to develop and retain them. Marketing managers have to attract, improve the profitability of and retain customers. If you think in terms of only two of these tasks then you will miss vital opportunities.

To overcome the limitation of thinking in twos try drawing a triangle to remind you to think of a third possibility for every new problem or opportunity.

This new lens (L2) can also be used to make brainstorming more effective. Send out a brief 24 hours before your brainstorming session and ask every participant to bring along three ideas. If you have ten people and everyone does their idea homework, in the first few minutes you could potentially have 30 new ideas.

Application

Select a problem and place it in the middle of your page within a triangle. Try to develop at least three distinct solutions to the problem.

For example:

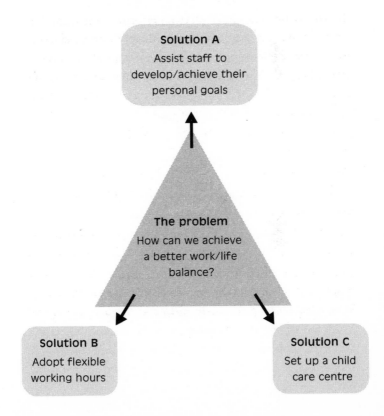

2

TOOL

Restate your goal in emotional language

Most goals or challenges are framed in a rational way—for example, 'How can we increase our market share by 5 per cent?' This often leads to small and incremental solutions. To bring about a new set of ideas, try redefining your goal (P2) in emotional language. Use words like 'passion', 'energy', 'fun', 'excite' and 'engage' when you reframe your problem. This will increase your chances of creating an imaginative solution.

For example, I worked with a software company that was about to launch a new product. Their stated objective was to obtain a 20 per cent unprompted awareness of their new product among their target audience. While this made sense it led to a range of familiar ideas. To push the group out of their comfort zone I encouraged them to redefine their challenge as 'How can we have our latest product talked about at dinner parties?' This opened their thinking and led to an array of bigger ideas.

Ask yourself, 'Which of these two challenges would I rather work on? Which challenge leads to a greater chance of new ideas and solutions?' For most of us the second one is the preferred option. The key to creating more innovative solutions is to keep the challenge or goal essentially the same but to use more expressive and engaging language.

Application

Focus on a particular problem you are currently facing (P1). Develop five possible solutions. Then redefine the problem using emotional language (P2) and create five new solutions. Select the most original response and test it.

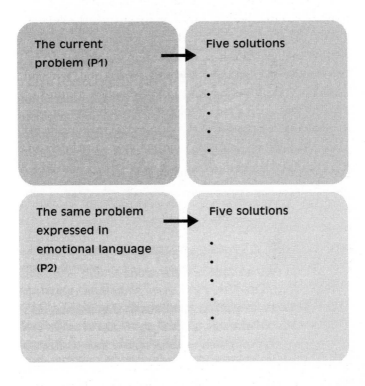

3

TOOL

Find new measurements

When solving a problem, you are often a prisoner of the measurements you use. For example, market share movements, while useful, are a reactive measure. They tell you what has happened rather than predicting what might occur in the future.

The measurements you use also tend to limit the possible solutions to a problem. By changing or adding a new array of measurements you can open yourself up to a new view of the problem (L2) and possibly a new range of solutions. Remember that measurements or key performance indicators can be both objective or subjective.

For example, consider the problem, 'How can we improve the satisfaction of employees?' One way of assessing this might be the number of days staff are absent. But what about another, complementary, measure such as the level of passion in the workforce? For instance, ask staff how passionately they feel about their job or the company? To be sure, this measure is more subjective, but it provides another more expansive way of defining the problem.

Application

Write down the current problem and the typical way you measure the solutions to this problem.

Now consider a number of new measurements for this same problem. Next, create some new ideas to tackle the original problem using the new measurements.

For example:

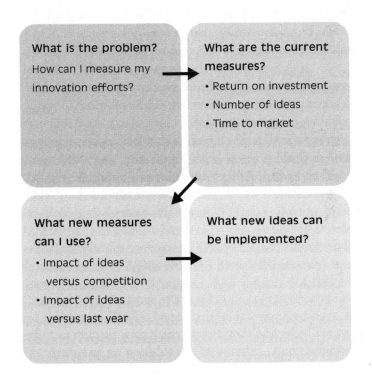

4

TOOL

Create new eyes

This is a very effective way of bringing about a new range of solutions. Using this tool, deliberately consider a problem from a number of different perspectives (L2).

Each one of us has a different perspective or lens, based on our assumptions, values, beliefs and experiences. And while we can never know how someone really sees a situation, we can imagine how they might perceive a problem or challenge.

For example, if you are about to make an important new business call to a potential client, you should consider who might be at the meeting and what their lens could be. The managing director, for example, might see the situation in terms of long-term growth opportunities, while the sales director might be more interested in the short-term impact on sales. By imagining your clients' different perspectives (L2s) you can better tailor your message to the way they see the situation.

Application

Select a letter at random. If you selected 'a', think of a role, person or animal starting with this letter—for example, an astronaut. Now consider the problem (P1) from a range of different perspectives (L2s) using this letter.

Then ask yourself, 'How would an architect or accountant look at this problem?' Write down as many responses as you can in the next few minutes.

For example:

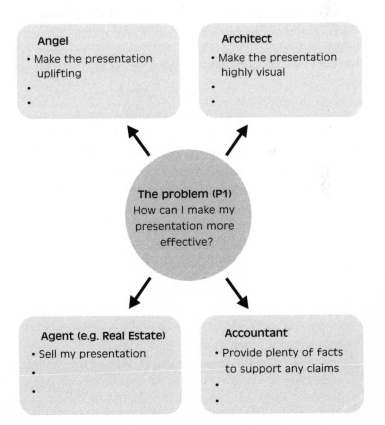

Angel
• Make the presentation uplifting
•
•

Architect
• Make the presentation highly visual
•
•

The problem (P1)
How can I make my presentation more effective?

Agent (e.g. Real Estate)
• Sell my presentation
•
•

Accountant
• Provide plenty of facts to support any claims
•
•

TOOL

Develop a range of business-as-usual, different and radical solutions

When faced with a problem (P1), try to develop a range of business-as-usual, different and radical solutions as quickly as you can. This new lens (L2) pushes you to develop a greater range of solutions and gives you permission to offer those really left-field ideas.

The business-as-usual solutions are a continuation of what has been done traditionally. The different solutions are a departure from what has gone on before. The radical solutions are a departure from what has been suggested before. Think big! Then select the best outcome (it could be one of the options or a combination of several).

For example, consider the problem, 'How do we retain our best managers?' A business-as-usual solution might be to pay high-performing managers more. A different approach could be to expand their responsibilities or move them to a new (perhaps struggling) department. A radical approach might be to provide them with a six-month sabbatical or give them a small company-owned business to run.

This framework is also a very powerful way of selling your ideas. It is a good way of providing the client with real choice. Start by outlining the business-as-usual solution, then outline the different approach. Leave the radical one for last. Clients are often more willing to entertain the thought of a radical idea if they have the more bankable tried-and-true option on the table.

Application

Place the problem (P1) in the middle of the triangle, then try to develop five business-as-usual solutions, three different solutions and at least one radical solution in the next five minutes.

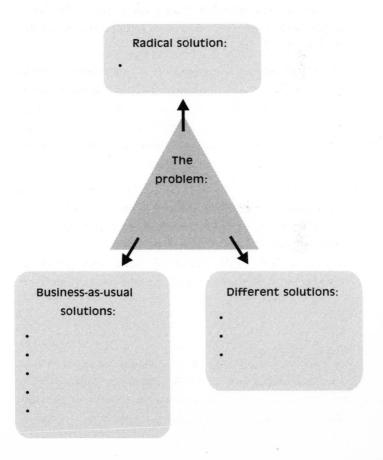

TOOL

6

Solve a bigger problem

A powerful way of bringing about a breakthrough solution is to make the current problem (P1) more encompassing.

We have a tendency to focus only on bite-sized problems but a new solution might emerge by concentrating on a larger problem (P2).

For example, instead of solving the problem, 'How can I improve the level of customer service?' (P1), expand it to be 'How can I enhance my customer's life?' (P2). This can open up the problem to many different ways of being solved. By broadening the problem you shift the focus away from how you sell the product or service to how your offering fits into the customer's life. This is a much stronger place from which to develop new ideas.

For example, if you have a brand aimed at kids, provide suggestions on how to make birthday parties fun for different ages. Kids and mums will love you.

Application

Write down your current problem (P1), then progressively make the problem bigger. Try to develop one new problem (P2) every couple of minutes. In ten minutes you will have at least five new problems. Select the one that is the most intriguing and create new solutions.

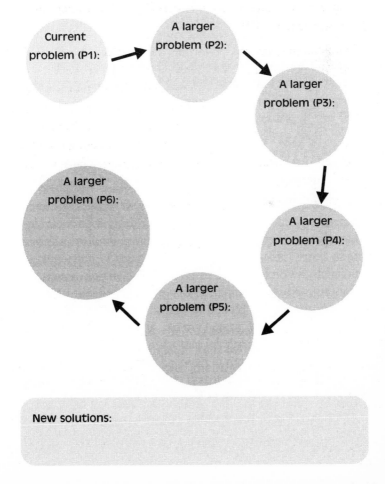

Current problem (P1):

A larger problem (P2):

A larger problem (P3):

A larger problem (P4):

A larger problem (P5):

A larger problem (P6):

New solutions:

TOOL

Ask new questions

When trying to solve a difficult problem, a good place to start is to ask a range of new questions. These are questions to which you genuinely do not know the answer. This is difficult initially, because we have been taught to concentrate on solving existing problems and not on creating more insightful questions.

The process of asking new questions can open up our thinking and help us to see the problem in a new light, which can lead to new answers.

For example, most business people face the challenge of trying to develop new products for a specific target audience. A new question might be, 'What customer experience would my customers rave about?' Asking new questions will often lead to better and more powerful solutions.

Application

Select a problem (P1) and in the next few minutes write all the existing questions you can think of about this problem.

Repeat the exercise, but now try to think of at least five new and varied questions. At this stage, don't try to answer them. The emphasis is on creating more original questions. Have a partner do the same.

Then compare the new questions, select the three that are the most interesting and try to solve them.

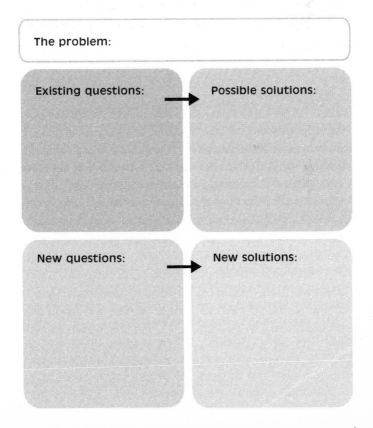

The problem:

Existing questions:

Possible solutions:

New questions:

New solutions:

TOOL

8

Find a solution that initially won't work

This is a counter-intuitive approach, because when you are looking at a difficult problem (P1) sometimes you have to escape from the usual or traditional solutions.

One way to achieve this is to develop a list of solutions that, on the surface, seem as if they won't work, then try to find a way to make them work. For example, 'What can I do to avoid having too much work and too little time?' A solution that would probably not make sense would be to add even more work. This might force you to become more ruthless in your priorities, consider sharing some of the load, or learn how to think faster. Making a problem worse can sometimes bring out a more original solution.

An example of this method in action is the following. Consider the question, 'How can we improve our product quality?' A typical solution would include reviewing the current process to identify defects. A counter-intuitive approach would be to deliberately limit product quality, leading to a cheaper price and perhaps new market opportunities.

Application

This is a good exercise to do with a partner. Select a problem, then in the next five minutes write down as many workable solutions as you can and how you might implement them. Repeat the exercise, but this time have each person develop at least five 'unworkable' solutions. Then swap ideas and try to find new solutions to make them more workable.

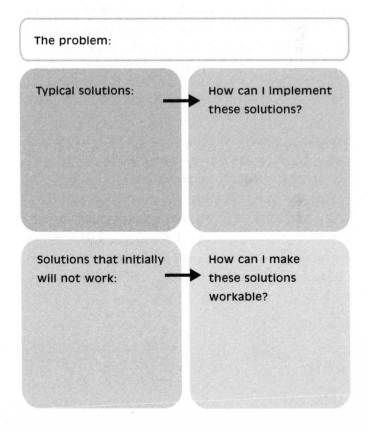

The problem:

Typical solutions:

→ How can I implement these solutions?

Solutions that initially will not work:

→ How can I make these solutions workable?

9

TOOL

Use a new simile

When faced with a problem (P1) try using a new simile. The simile you often unconsciously use can limit your potential solutions. For example, the dominant simile used in business is 'this business runs like a well-oiled machine'. This simile conveys efficiency and punctuality. But thinking of your business in this way can limit your approach, because it doesn't lend itself to experimentation or risk-taking.

To bring about a breakthrough solution, try to change the problem by varying the simile in your business. By changing the simile, you can often design new possibilities.

For example, if you are trying to obtain an interview with a potential client, but their personal assistant is putting up barriers to the meeting (like a locked door), using a new simile might provide an answer. If you see this problem as 'like flying a kite', it might lead you to these possible solutions:

- engage in a conversation with the PA—what are they interested in? (i.e. what are their emotional strings?)
- invite the potential client and the PA to lunch (i.e. like flying a kite together).

Application

Select a problem (P1). Then think of a number of different similes (the more unrelated the better). Use at least two of these at random in the next five minutes to create a range of new solutions.

The problem:

The current simile:

A new simile:

Possible new solutions:

For example:
This problem is 'like a circus'

- Can I make the solution colourful?
- Can music be used?
- Where is the drama in the solution?

For example:
This problem is 'like an orchestra'

- Do we have a diverse range of voices and sounds?
- Do we need a new leader or conductor?
- Are there other departments that can help?

10

TOOL

Find a paradox

Some seemingly intractable problems (P1) are difficult to solve because they contain paradoxes. Our usual reaction is to avoid these paradoxes but they are often the source of new ideas and solutions. Think how the famous 'less is more' paradox in architecture has been applied to designing new furniture and other space-saving equipment.

To create a new problem (P2) try to uncover any potential paradoxes in the problem before you. For example, consider the problem, 'Why is my breakfast brand losing sales?' A possible paradox in addressing this problem might be 'busy people are too busy to eat breakfast'. This might be solved by developing new, more convenient breakfast formats, such as breakfast bars or breakfast on wheels (similar to mobile coffee carts) or developing an office breakfast delivery service.

Consider another paradox: a successful business is some-times more likely to be unsuccessful. Why? Because successful business leaders can become complacent and resistant to change. Thus they need to be aggressively open to new ideas.

Application

Select a problem, then think of at least three paradoxes inherent in this problem. Try to create five new ways of potentially resolving each of these paradoxes. Select the most effective solution from the second column and try to test it.

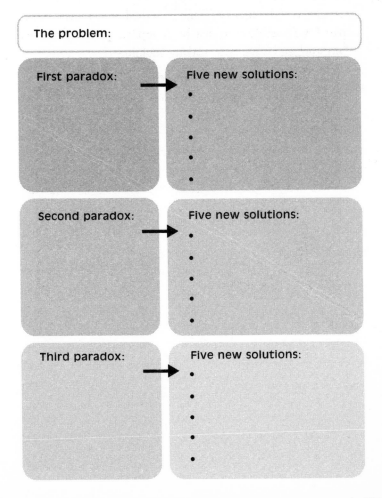

The problem:

First paradox:

Five new solutions:
-
-
-
-
-

Second paradox:

Five new solutions:
-
-
-
-
-

Third paradox:

Five new solutions:
-
-
-
-
-

'Imagination is more important than

knowledge.'

Albert Einstein

2 TEN TOOLS TO CREATE NEW GROWTH OPPORTUNITIES

TOOL

1

Study unrelated industries

Many managers only focus on companies in their industry or product category. Although being aware of what your competitors are doing is valuable, it can lead to a 'me too' approach.

To create a new view of your opportunities (L2) you need to explore what is happening in other industries—the more unrelated the better. For example, a few brands in the airline industry are now offering, 'Pay for ten flights and get the next one free.' This type of proposition has been common in the retail industry for a long time but is new to the airline industry.

The practice of studying unrelated industries can give you a jump on your competitors and create a pipeline of innovative new ideas. With some adaptation, a successful idea from another industry can be applied to your own.

What ideas can you learn, adapt or borrow from other unrelated industries?

Application

Pick up a business magazine or the daily newspaper. Select a completely unrelated category or industry to the one you are working in.

Then select an interesting product or service from that industry and try to apply it to your business. Remember to concentrate on the core of the idea, not the execution. Repeat this practice every month. In twelve months you will have initiatives from a vast range of new sources at your fingertips.

For example:

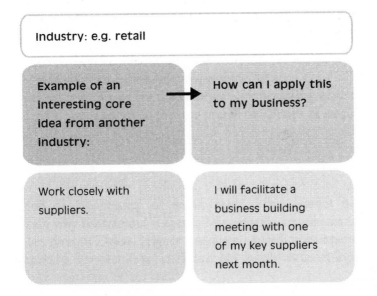

TOOL

2

Design the perfect customer experience

The traditional approach to improving customer service is to ask your customer to rate their experience of using your product through some form of customer satisfaction survey.

This approach has its place but often leads to incremental enhancements, because you can become stuck continuing the current system. To create a leap in performance you will need to use a different lens (L2).

Imagine what the perfect customer experience feels like.[1] For example, I can imagine a post office that is a joy to visit. It is a place that is friendly, helpful and full of surprises. This is a long way from most people's experiences as they line up at a post office waiting to be served.

Once you have created the perfect scenario you can compare and contrast the ideal one with the current situation. Where are the gaps and how can you address these?

Application

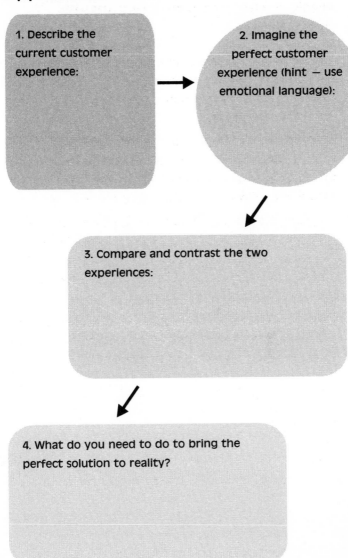

1. Describe the current customer experience:

2. Imagine the perfect customer experience (hint — use emotional language):

3. Compare and contrast the two experiences:

4. What do you need to do to bring the perfect solution to reality?

TOOL 3

Place two unrelated things together

Arthur Koestler once suggested that the creative act consists of placing two unrelated items together.[2] This process can be used to disrupt your conventional view of a situation (L1) and creates a new lens (L2) through which you must try to make a connection between two seemingly distinct ideas.

For example, it was only a few years ago that someone had the idea of combining a café with a car-wash, allowing customers to enjoy a coffee while they waited for their car to be cleaned. There is nothing original about a café or a car-wash, but placing these two things together was a breakthrough and a profitable business idea.

The magic in using this tool is to place genuinely unrelated things together. For example, as shown in the application, it could be a potential new customer segment (teenagers) alongside an existing distribution channel (university).

Application

A good way to use this tool is to draw two intersecting axes. Then ask yourself what would happen if you combined factor x with factor y. Explore the new opportunity space that is created.

Drawing the two axes is a very powerful, visual way of creating a new opportunity. In the example below, perhaps there is an opportunity to change the education policy by having Year 11 school kids attend university for a month so they know if university is right for them.

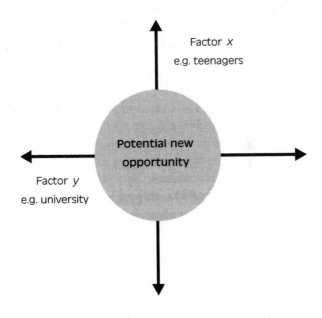

Factor x
e.g. teenagers

Potential new opportunity

Factor y
e.g. university

TOOL

4

Become one of your competitors

The traditional way of analysing the competition is to consider their actions from the perspective of your business (L1). This is an 'inside out' perspective, which lacks insight and does not provide any clues as to what the competition may do in the future.

To bring about a shift in perspective (L2) imagine yourself as one of your competitors. Then ask yourself, 'What actions will I undertake in the next 12 months? What new products will I launch? What potential new channels can I test?'

Looking at your business from the competitor's perspective helps you to better anticipate your competitor's actions, and hopefully gain an edge.

This is a very good tool to use with a larger group, as smaller teams can imagine themselves as different competitors. For example, a few years ago I worked with a management team at a charge-card company, and by playing around with different competitive mindsets they realised that their biggest future competitor was not other credit or charge cards, but EFTPOS and ATM cards. This larger competitive threat had been largely ignored.

Application

One of the best ways to apply this tool is to chart your current, future, direct and indirect competitors. For example, if you ran a domestic airline your current direct competitors would be other airlines, an indirect competitor could be a bus company, a future direct competitor could be a private jet company (particularly if it focused on business travellers) and a future indirect competitor might be a company such as GE, who might decide to move into the airline business.

The first step is to outline who the competitors might be and then imagine their actions in the next 12 months. Spend five minutes on each competitor.

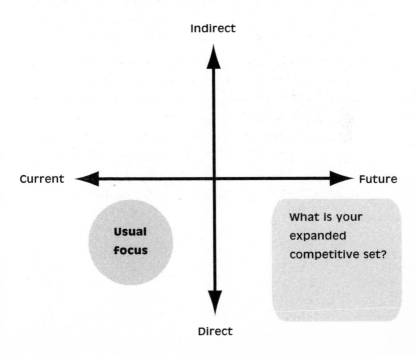

TOOL

5

Imagine your future landscape

A good way to create a new growth opportunity is to imagine what your operating landscape might be in three to five years' time. This allows you to see opportunities that you can take advantage of before your competition steps in.

It is important to use three to five years as your yardstick, because it allows you to consider a broader range of possibilities. If you use a shorter time frame it is difficult to escape your current lens (L1), which may only look a year ahead at a time.

When you have imagined a future landscape, ask yourself where you would like your brand and/or business to be positioned. Who will your competitors be? What will consumers want?

By using this information you can start to build a new range of growth opportunities. For example, if you were running a business selling printers, you might consider a scenario where young people are more likely to buy products that are cool or hip. This might lead you to have a merger with, for instance, a surf brand (e.g. Billabong) that might want to extend their brand in a completely new direction.

Application

Capture your current environment in the table below. Then imagine a different competitive landscape in three to five years' time. How will it differ? How might you respond given these two different scenarios?

What is your competitive landscape?		
Dimension	Current situation	In three to five years
Customers		
Competition		
Channels		
Margins		
Suppliers		

The next step is to consider an abrupt change to one of the dimensions. It might be a change in a law or a completely new competitor. Again consider how you might respond and what opportunities might emerge.

TOOL

6

Become a fashion brand

An effective way to create a new growth opportunity is to start thinking of your brand or business as a fashion brand. This new lens (L2) means that you have to stay up to date with the latest trends and fashion from around the world and apply it to your business or brand.

For example, think about how mobile phones have become fashion statements. Or how portable music systems have become fashion accessories.

Your brand or business can create new opportunities simply by starting to think about itself as a fashion brand. Are you up to date with the latest fashions, or are you simply following the trends?

How can your brand or business become a fashion leader?

Application

Think of as many fashion brands as you can in the next few minutes. Consider both male and female fashion brands. Here are some to get you started:

- YSL
- Sass & Bide
- Nokia
- Apple
- Chanel
- Armani

Now select a brand. What can you learn from the fashionable aspects of this brand? How does the brand stay relevant? How does the brand change between different national markets?

Who is the fashion leader in your industry? Could your brand take this position? How could a bank, for example, make itself fashionable?

7

TOOL

Make your product beautiful

The next time you go shopping, visit the consumer electronic section. Have a close look at the toasters and washing machines. The traditional view is that these types of products have to be functional in appearance. A new lens says that these types of products should also be beautiful to look at.

If your products are pleasing to the eye as well as high quality, then you have gained a real advantage over your competitors.

Design is the new expectation of every consumer across every industry. Beautiful design can differentiate your product and increase sales and margins.

How can you make your product beautiful to look at without sacrificing functionality or performance?

Application

Here are some suggestions to make your range of products beautiful.

- Hire an industrial designer or interior decorator to look at your product range.
- Hold a design competition for your employees to contribute ideas.
- Ask the consumers for ways to improve the design of an existing product or for feedback on the design of a new product.
- Visit a museum or art gallery and study the artworks for design ideas.
- Study the design of a range of products from an unrelated industry.
- Talk to a number of award-winning architects.

What can you learn, borrow or adapt from these actions?

TOOL

8

Get a win/win

Your business suppliers and partners are an ideal and often under-utilised source of new growth opportunities. Many managers are locked into a dated, cost-based mindset, which can lead to acrimonious negotiations that are limited in scope to price or trading terms.

A more productive approach is to redefine the problem (P2) as 'How can we both win?'

I recently conducted a session with a wine company and one of their key suppliers. At the beginning of the session I outlined the rules of the game—we could only create ideas that would benefit both parties. If the idea did not deliver a win/win then it could not be considered. This simple change of the ground rules opened up the interaction to an increased range of more original possibilities as both parties searched for new ways to grow both businesses. They eventually developed a proposition around speed of service, which both parties thought was a neglected market opportunity, and could lead to higher margins.

Application

Conduct a quarterly business-building session with each of your key clients, partners and suppliers.

The aim is to develop new propositions that benefit both businesses.

Be very explicit from the start as to what constitutes a 'win' for each party. With these two 'wins' in mind, the combined group can start to create new possibilities.

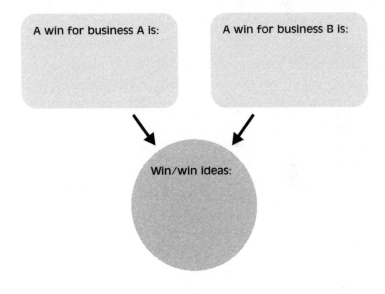

9

Consider the 'never evers'

People in business are constantly wrestling with the challenge of how to make their products more attractive to a specific, defined group of customers. This focused approach makes sense, but can limit potential growth opportunities as you are only concentrating on a limited market. However, with only a few minor adjustments, your product might be appealing to a different group, thus expanding your potential audience.

Try changing the problem to 'Who are the people that never buy our product and what could we offer them?' For example, at present all the mobile phone companies are designing phones that are small and stylish. But this leaves a potential market segment open. Why not consider a mobile phone for the mature-aged market? This market has money and time to learn about the new technology. A major appeal of this phone could be as a portable safety device with built-in safety numbers—it might also have a larger face or better speakers. It doesn't make good business sense for all the phone brands to compete for the same target audience and ignore other, potentially lucrative, markets.

Application

List at least six groups of people who *never* or *rarely* buy your product. Try to make the groups as interesting as possible.

For example:

- the unemployed
- the visually impaired
- those who speak English as a second language
- the under-tens
- single-parent households
- backpackers.

If you are working with a large group, allocate each of the potential customer segments you come up with to a small group and ask them to build a new proposition. For example, if you owned a gym, you could set up a specially priced membership where entry is restricted to several hours in the mid-morning and mid-afternoon—quiet business hours that would be available to the unemployed.

After building a proposition for their allocated group, each group should present and decide on the best offer. Try to test it in the next three to six months.

TOOL

10

Expand your usage occasions

This tool builds on Tool 9. A typical problem that managers grapple with is how to maximise the consumption of a product in a specific usage occasion—for example, cereal at breakfast. By defining the problem in this way you are limiting your thinking—you have already decided when and how consumers could use your product.

To escape this boundary, you need to create a new problem definition (P2). What are some new usage occasions that you have never considered? For example, think of how McDonald's has been trying to drive its business growth in the last ten years. One of the initiatives it has adopted has been to increase the number of usage occasions it provides to its customer base—for example, breakfast menus, McCafé and drive-through.

If your customer base is not growing, it makes sense to try to increase the number of usage occasions.

What potential usage opportunities might be available to your business?

Application

List at least five to seven potential usage occasions for your product or business that you haven't considered in the past. Don't try to evaluate them—simply try to create as many as you can.

For example:

- a day at the beach
- an afternoon cup of tea
- taking the dog for a walk
- brunch
- a Saturday night dinner party
- an after-dinner snack
- watching your kids play sport on Saturday.

If you are working with a larger group, have a smaller team work on each of these usage occasions. Each team has to design a new usage proposition and present it to the larger group. Ask the team with the best proposition to develop an action plan of how to test the new approach in the next 90 days.

'I believe that my creative mind is my

greatest weapon.'

Tiger Woods, *How I Play Golf*

3 TEN TOOLS TO IMMEDIATELY IMPROVE YOUR PERFORMANCE

TOOL

1

Create a new lens to view failure

One of the most paralysing barriers to high performance is the fear of failure. Many managers hold the perception that failing to achieve your goals should be avoided at all costs. This can mean that calculated risks are rarely taken and only sure-fire bets are entertained. This leads to incremental growth (personal and business) and a 'follow the leader' mentality.

One way to break free of this mindset is to adopt a new lens (L2) that views failure as an opportunity to learn and grow. By doing this, failure isn't seen in such a negative way, and a more positive view of personal and business growth is established.

The aim in any successful business is to create a culture where everyone is encouraged to continually try new things, occasionally fail, but always push the boundaries of high performance.

Application

Using a different lens to view failure is just one example of how you can change your performance by changing your thinking.[1] You cannot control the event—for example, a job transfer—but you can control how you interpret the event. By focusing on your own attitudes and beliefs, you can develop a more positive outlook on business and on life generally.

An effective practice of dealing with change is to write down your current lens (L1). Come up with a new way of viewing this change (L2), then commit to a new set of actions that might flow from this new lens.

For example:

The event	Possible retrenchment
What is my current lens?	'I fear the unknown.'
What is a new lens?	'This might be an opportunity to try something new.'
What new behaviour will result?	'I will talk to other people who have been retrenched.'

TOOL 2

View risk-taking as a normal part of business

Related to the fear of failure is the practice of taking risks. I have found that high-performing people tend to take more calculated risks or, perhaps more accurately, they view taking risks as an integral part of doing business.

At one large pharmaceutical company, for example, the CEO is constantly reminding his team that trial and error is an integral part of the innovative process. Taking more risks means that you can gain an edge on your competition. It can also open up new growth opportunities.

Think of some of the major achievements in your life outside of work (e.g. getting married, travelling overseas)—didn't these involve some degree of risk?

To become a high-performing employee or manager means applying the same sort of mindset you apply to your personal life to your business career.

Application

Identify all the possible risks around a decision. Determine how you can decrease this risk and what the consequences are if you fail.

Armed with this knowledge, you are in a better position to see if the risk is worth taking. The simple practice of making a risk factor explicit also helps you deal with it.

For example:

Decision or issue:		
Risk factor	**How can I reduce the risk factor?**	**What is the worst scenario?**
Changing careers.	Talk to other people who have changed careers.	It might be difficult to go back to my original career.

TOOL 3

Adopt a test mindset

High performers are constantly experimenting with new ideas and approaches. They do not accept the status quo (L1). Rather they adopt a mindset of continual experimentation.

An experimental mindset (L2) encourages you to take more risks and to try new things, knowing that it is only a test. For example, the award-winning animated movie company Pixar tests most of their new technologies on their shorter films before applying them to full-length movies.

The benefit of continually testing new ideas is that you can see what works and what doesn't before rolling it out. Remember, these do not have to be big things, but you need to be constantly pushing the envelope.

My suggestion is for everyone to be testing three new things at any one point in time.

Application

To provide a focus for your testing strategy, nominate your top five priorities.

Select one at random and then design some simple, quick and cheap ways of testing a range of new approaches that address one of these key priorities.

For example:

What are my key priorities?	How can I test the new approach?
To improve my people-management skills.	Take my team out for lunch to say thanks and to discuss ways of improving the business.

4

TOOL

Change the way you view your barriers to success

It is time for an honest assessment of your performance in the past 12 months—what golfer Greg Norman calls 'the mirror test'. You can fool others, but not yourself.

Take a good, hard look at yourself and determine what is holding you back. Ask yourself, 'What barriers to performance do I need to overcome to unlock my true potential? How do I view these barriers (L1)?' Write it all down. Sometimes the process of making these things explicit can bring about a change in performance.

In my case, it was my new business pipeline. I viewed finding new business as hard work, which often meant that my pipeline of new leads ran low. I needed to admit that my perception of the situation was what was holding me back, and that I needed to create a new lens. My new business work really turned around when I started to view finding leads as a great adventure (L2). It led to a more aggressive new business strategy and the hiring of a public relations company to promote my business. The improvement in results was almost instantaneous.

Application

Talk with a trusted friend or colleague, or perhaps someone outside your business who is likely to be objective and have a fresh perspective. Tell them about your achievements over the last year and the barriers that have been blocking your path to success. Be clear and specific about the barriers. After these have been identified, select a few at random and try to articulate how you view these barriers (i.e. your L1).

Next try to develop a new lens (L2) to view these barriers. Then develop a range of action steps that flow from this new perspective. When you have worked your way through your barriers, have your friend or colleague reciprocate the arrangement.

The benefit of this approach is that your friend or colleague might offer a new perspective and help you overcome your barriers to success.

For example:

What are my barriers?	What is my current lens?	What is my new lens?
I am not very good at giving presentations.	I feel nervous speaking in front of people.	This is a new opportunity to expand my skills.

TOOL

5

Set a breakthrough challenge

The challenge you set yourself often limits your expectations. If you expect a 3 per cent improvement, you will feel satisfied if you deliver this.

Most of us are content with improving on last year's results by only a few percentage points. This is fine as long as your competition plays by the same rules. What if they raise their performance by 40 per cent? You will be left behind.

To break free of this incremental cycle, set yourself a breakthrough or impossible challenge (P2). The challenge should be very specific to the area that is key to your performance. For example, it could be in your sales results, your people skills or in your dealings with customers.

It doesn't matter what area you focus on. Your performance will lift because you have established a new, higher benchmark of performance and expectations—much like when Roger Bannister broke the four-minute mile. Many others smashed this barrier soon after.

Application

List all of your major responsibilities in the table below. From this list, highlight those in which your performance has improved only slightly in the last 12 months, and those in which you have delivered exceptional results. Rely on your gut feeling to make this assessment if you need to.

Focus on the incremental improvement areas. Then ask yourself, 'How can I make a giant leap in performance?'

For example:

What are my key responsibilities?	What areas have only improved incrementally?	How can I make a giant leap in performance?
People management	Providing timely feedback.	I will encourage my team to try some new things.

6

Improve your self-talk

Something that business people can learn from their sporting cousins is the importance athletes place on developing strong and vibrant self-talk.[2] Changing your self-talk from predominantly negative to more positive is a very powerful way of bringing about a lift in performance.

Your self-talk is the private conversation that occurs inside your head. This self-talk can be both positive (e.g. that was a real improvement) or negative (e.g. that mistake is typical; you are hopeless at this). The important point is that you can choose which one it will be.

My wife recently became discouraged about her work. I noticed that her self-talk was becoming more and more negative and absolute ('I am useless' rather than 'I made a mistake; I will do better next time'). She was not aware of this and when I mentioned it there was an immediate effect. She consciously tried to use more positive and forgiving self-talk, leaving her feeling better and more energised about her job.

Being more aware of your self-talk can have an immediate influence on your mood and energy levels.

Application

Record your self-talk over a week by using the table below. Is it positive, encouraging and tolerant of mistakes? Or is it negative? I have found that we are often our own biggest critic.

The challenge is to be alert to our self-talk and try to bring about a lift in performance by changing the existing lens (L1) into a more positive one (L2). It is also beneficial to make your self-talk specific to a situation rather than making a general statement. For example, if you do not handle a situation with your son or daughter very well, it doesn't necessarily make you a bad parent; it just provides you with a learning experience to help you become a better one.

For example:

What is my current self-talk lens?	What is my new self-talk lens?
I am not as successful as I should be.	My performance is improving; success will come if I keep at it.

7

TOOL

Make your 'lens in use' explicit

One way for you to have a dramatic impact on your performance is to challenge, stretch or break free of your business or industry conventions.

These collective conventions are often unstated, but become the 'unwritten rules of the game' that everyone tends to follow. For example, there are often conventions about how to earn profit, how to distribute products or which markets are profitable.

However, these conventions are often due to the fact that every manager is viewing the industry in the same way. They are all using the same lens (L1). But these boundaries are mindset ones—assumptions or beliefs—rather than marketplace ones, and therefore can be challenged.

Business leaders who can bring about a collective new view of their category or industry (an L2) can often create an advantage. Apple challenged the convention that computers must look functional with the launch of their beautiful Apple Mac computers. Virgin regularly challenges conventions as they enter new industries.

If you can break free of your industry mindset, you can stay ahead of your competition.

Application

I have found one of the most effective ways to begin challenging conventions is to make them explicit. Using the model below, list the assumptions, beliefs, conventions and experiences of trying to grow a specific brand or business.

Then select one of these at random and try to stretch it and/or break free of it. For example, if every competitor is using television can you use another medium, such as radio and/or the internet?

Conventions:
Every competitor uses television advertising.

Assumptions:
We assume that our retailers will support our growth initiatives.

What is your growth mindset for your brand or business?

Beliefs:
We have better ideas than the competition.

Experiences:
We do not tolerate a growth initiative that is unprofitable in the short term.

8

Understand the other person's mindset

To get the best out of another person, a valuable starting point is to try to understand their view of the world (their L1).

If you can see a situation from their point of view, you can customise your message and help them to overcome any perceived barriers. We often spend too much time trying to convince others of our point of view and become frustrated when they fail to embrace our position.

Everyone sees the world differently, which is what gives society its great diversity. There is no one best way to see a situation. For example, when he was a political prisoner, former South African president Nelson Mandela started all his correspondence with the government authorities by stating how difficult it must be to make any decision about his situation. This demonstration of empathy and emotional intelligence made the process of reconciliation so much easier for all when he eventually became president.

Application

This is another adaptation of the mindset tool used in Tool 7 but instead of using it to break free of a convention, it is used to increase your understanding of a situation from another person's view—for example, when you are applying for a promotion or a new role.

The task here is to make explicit what you believe are the assumptions, conventions, experiences and beliefs the person has of a particular situation—for example, the interview. Do this quickly without agonising over it. This way you can compare their view with yours and start to address their issues in a proactive way.

For example:

Their conventions:
Every competitor uses television advertising.

Their assumptions:
There can only be one person promoted.

The other person's view of a situation

Their beliefs:
You are competing with me for a promotion.

Their experiences:
People who excel in their job are more likely to be promoted.

TOOL 9

Develop a radical new goal for every process that is two years old

We are caught up in one process or another for most of our working life. Depending on the size of the organisation we work in, there are processes for developing new products, or receiving accounts, for example. Processes provide order, clarity and structure. However, over time some processes can become rigid and outdated and end up being a barrier to change and innovation.

A way to escape this organisational rigidity is to set up a radical challenge (a new P2) for a specific process and then redesign the process to meet this new challenge.

A high-performing person aims to change a process to suit them rather than become a victim of it. For example, rather than relying only on the high school test score to admit potential students into medical school, some universities are enhancing this process by adding in additional requirements, such as interviews, hospital visits and information sessions with doctors. This keeps the student recruitment process relevant for both the university and the potential student.

Application

List a number of different processes that you are involved with as quickly as you can. Then select one at random.

Set yourself a big, new challenge (P2): for example, 'How can we halve the time it takes to test new products?' Then complete the exercise below by writing down how you would use the current process to meet the challenge, and how the process could be redesigned to meet the challenge more effectively.

Radical process outcome:		
	What is the current process?	How can it be radically redesigned?
Who?		
When?		
What?		
Where?		
Why?		
How?		

TOOL

10

Do a few things exceptionally well

Most of us are incredibly busy. We are all trying to do multiple jobs with limited time. That is why this book has been written—to help you think in a quicker and more powerful way so that you can make the most of the time you have available.

However, to escape a cycle of half-completed projects, you need to become ruthless about your priorities. It is more important to do a few jobs really well than to do a lot of jobs moderately well. This requires a change in mindset from 'I must do everything reasonably well' to 'I must do a few things exceptionally well'.

As Apple founder Steve Jobs notes, 'Innovation comes from saying no to 1000 things to make sure we don't get on the wrong track or try to do too much. We're always thinking about new markets we could enter, but it is only by saying no that you could concentrate on the things that are really important.'[3]

Application

To bring about a lift in performance, imagine you have only six months left in your job. What is truly important to you now? What will you concentrate on? How can you make a difference in the shortest possible time? What would you most want to be remembered for?

Be absolutely single-minded on the most important project facing you. Delegate or reorder your priorities so that you have enough time to achieve your goals in the manner you want.

What is my current list of priorities?	What is my biggest priority?	How can I move it forward?

'Nothing drives progress like the

imagination. The idea precedes the deed.'

Theodore Levitt, *Marketing Imagination*

TEN TOOLS TO ENHANCE YOUR TEAM'S PERFORMANCE

TOOL

1

Push the team out of its comfort zone

Teams often develop a collective lens (or L1) that represents a kind of group comfort zone. To achieve outstanding team performance, it is sometimes necessary to move the team out of its collective comfort zone by introducing the members to new experiences. For example, move people around, give them different roles or halve the time the team has been given to complete a project. These experiences mean that the collective lens is shattered and a new lens (L2) emerges.

Sometimes teams can go where individual members dare not tread, and a team may be more willing to take a collective risk to move the business forward.

For example, many people who are embarking on a new fitness campaign find that working with others in a 'boot camp' provides effective results. Being yelled at by a fitness drill sergeant is an experience most people would avoid if they were by themselves, but might tolerate in a group environment.

Application

Divide your team into two smaller groups.

Select a key business challenge and ask each of the teams to write down six actions that would address this challenge, but make them feel uncomfortable. For example, if the issue was how to better understand the customer, the uncomfortable action might be to spend a day in the field with the sales team making new business calls.

Concentrate on the uncomfortable list and select one for the next month. Remember to swap lists so that team A has team B's uncomfortable list. This ensures that the team members are collectively moving out of their comfort zone.

What is my key business challenge?	What are some actions that address this challenge but are uncomfortable to perform?

TOOL

2

Study a great team outside business

To learn how to achieve a higher team performance, you sometimes need to look outside the business environment.[1] For example, think of a sporting team that has delivered sustained high performance, such as the Australian women's swimming team.

By studying a non-business team you can break free of the usual lens (L1) and develop a new lens (L2) to discover what high performance means in a different context.

One of the lessons the Australian swimming team, for example, learned was that female swimmers often need to be coached in a different way to male swimmers.

If you look at your organisation or team, would you be better served by having your up-and-coming female leaders coached or mentored by other females?

Application

One of the most effective ways to get your team to open up to the idea of studying other great teams is for each of your team members to reflect upon their own life experiences. Ask each team member to list the characteristics of a great team that they have been a part of. It could be a sense of common purpose, diverse people, or something else entirely. What worked and why? Doing this reinforces the idea that building a high-performing team is within anyone's reach.

After the group has decided which characteristics from their list are the most important, search for a great, non-business team that typifies these characteristics.

What great team have you been a part of?	What can you learn, adapt or borrow from this team?

TOOL

3

Build the most diverse team you can imagine

One of the secrets of high-performing teams is that they are comprised of people with a diverse range of skills and life experiences. Diverse teams have a broad array of individual lenses, which when combined can create more original solutions.

Try designing a team based entirely on difference. In effect, you are trying to design a team where there is initially nothing in common. This is very different from the usual approach, which is to bring together people that have something in common, such as a similar background, education or functional experience.

In a truly diverse team, members will soon realise that there are many different ways of solving any problem, and the creative interactions that follow often result in a more effective solution.

The challenge, however, is ensuring that people with diverse mindsets still value, respect and listen to one another. If not, you will have diversity but no common goals.

Application

To ensure that your team has a diversity of perspectives, rate all members according to their preferred intelligence styles.[2] These styles are present in all of us to varying degrees. In a truly diverse team, you should have a mixture of people who prefer using their rational, emotional or imaginative intelligence most of the time.

What intelligence type best describes the members of your team?

- People with rational intelligence prefer to use logic, analysis and reason.
- People with emotional intelligence prefer working with people in a collaborative way. These people provide energy and passion.
- People with creative intelligence prefer to create new solutions and challenge the status quo.

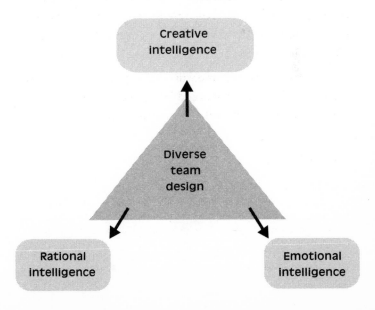

TOOL

4

Build a great team from the individual up

Increasingly, the team is seen as the main driver of organisational change. Leaders have formed cross-functional teams, new product development teams and innovation teams, to name just a few.

The emphasis on team work does have a downside, however. It can mean that the individual, original thinker can become lost or marginalised. Can you imagine someone like Albert Einstein working in your business? Job advertisements today usually state that the person must be a team player. But the focus on the team can mean that more introverted members, and those at the bottom of the totem pole, can be silenced.

A new way of thinking about team design (L2) is to build a great team from the individual up. Select one high-performing individual, then decide who else could add value to them. Then add another person to the mix until you have the desired number of team members.

Application

Listed below are some effective ways to build a more productive team from the individual up.

1. Start your next idea session by asking everyone to solve a problem by themselves in the first five minutes. There is to be no talking during this time. Then have each person work with a partner and present the pair's best ideas to the larger group.

2. Hold a problem-solving contest between the individual members of the group. Post a problem and ask each group member to try to develop as many different solutions as possible in five minutes. Then compare and contrast the ideas within the group.

3. When you are evaluating an idea, give everyone three ticks to place against any of the ideas created. Each member can vote for a single idea with all three ticks, or spread them around. Give the team only 60 seconds to decide so they have to use their intuition. You can then focus the meeting around the best ideas as voted by the group members.

TOOL

5

Think strategically and aim for quick wins

To build a high-performing team, members have to change their lens (L1) from 'we will generate short-term results *or* focus on the long term' to 'we must think strategically *and* obtain quick wins' (L2). The replacement of *or* with *and* sets up a new way of viewing the goals of the team.[3]

An early win is particularly beneficial to teams that have just formed. These wins give the team momentum and confidence. They also send a message to the remainder of the business that the team is up and running and already generating results.

For example, I was working with a despondent and frustrated revenue growth team in a manufacturing business. When we analysed the projects the group was working on, none of them was expected to generate any sort of payoff for 12 months. I suggested that it might be better to focus initially on some quicker projects. This resulted in greater energy and the acceptance of the group by the rest of the business.

Building a high-performing team means that short-term results must live alongside long-term strategic direction.

Application

The starting point for any team is to plot all the current and potential projects the team is working on or considering.

The aim is to have a balanced portfolio of projects—short, medium and long term. The matrix below will help with your efforts. If you have an unbalanced portfolio, then you should reconsider some of the projects. When a new initiative emerges it can be plotted, then compared and contrasted with the existing projects.

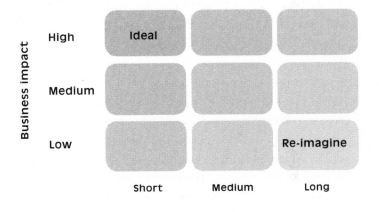

TOOL

6

Focus on being receptive to ideas

One of the quickest ways to enhance team performance is to increase the willingness of the group to accept new and different solutions. Often there are plenty of left-field ideas floating around but the group members aren't receptive. The aim in a high-performing team is to keep moving towards a goal and to create a team environment where all new ideas are listened to.

High team performance is predominantly driven by creating and sustaining the energy of its group members. When an idea is not listened to or curtailed prematurely, energy is sucked out of the group.

The best ideas often come from the most unexpected places and people. For example, I once worked with a brand team that was developing some new dessert products. A personal assistant, who was there to take notes, suggested a new product idea based on something she had seen overseas. Because the group was open to new ideas, they built upon the assistant's initial idea, and in the end it was voted the best of the workshop.

Application

Just as there are tools to generate new ideas, there are techniques than can help group members open up to new ideas.

I have listed two below:

1. Use 'yes *and*' not 'yes *but*'

Instead of using 'Yes I hear your idea *but* here is why your idea will not work', the group must use, 'Yes I understand your idea *and* here is how we can make the idea stronger'. People are often amazed at the difference in the interaction between the idea creator and the idea receiver.

2. Find something interesting about the idea

In this situation, the person receiving the idea has to find something interesting about the idea. This suspends initial judgement of the idea and encourages the person to really listen to the idea. The person proposing the idea is usually more willing to offer a left-field idea if they know that the other person is initially prepared to explore the idea.

TOOL

7

Form an 'out of the box' team

If you want to produce more creative ideas you often have to think in a non-linear way. There is no rule, for example, that every team has to be an implementation team.

A new way to think about non-linear or discontinuous innovation is to form a team of lateral thinkers who can develop new solutions to problems or create growth opportunities. This is a team of people who can make new connections or see new possibilities before they become apparent to others.

In a large insurance company I work with, the leaders have had tremendous success by forming a team like this. If someone is having a problem they brief this group, and the group creates a range of breakthrough solutions. The person with the problem is then free to test the new solutions.

The 'out of the box' team love working with other ideas people and feel genuinely valued.

If you do not work in a large business, try to form an 'out of the box' team with your colleagues, friends and/or suppliers and work on common problems.

Application

The key challenge when trying to form an 'out of the box' team is to identify the members. Remember, they can come from anywhere in the organisation.

I suggest two approaches:

1. Advertise for them

My consulting experience indicates that original thinkers often self-select themselves. By this I mean that you simply have to ask ten people and at least one (on average) will identify themselves as an 'out of the box' thinker. Hence you can post a note on your intranet or send an email asking for people who are lateral thinkers. The headline of the message, not surprisingly, should be 'Are you an "out of the box" thinker?'

2. Ask your peers to nominate

Another effective way to find the lateral thinkers in your business is to ask people to nominate those members of their department or team who can consistently develop left-field ideas.

TOOL 8

Define what winning means

In my experience, many teams form with no real idea how their efforts are to be judged. This places team members in a difficult situation, because they will not know if they are succeeding or not.

To avoid this, after the team is formed and the key objectives are established, the group should decide on what succeeding means before embarking on the project.

The members should decide the criteria on which the group will be judged in consultation with the leaders of the business. This means the team can to a large extent control its own destiny, which can be very motivating because the goal posts are clear.

There should be a range of objective criteria—for example, financial, skill development, meeting deadlines, and so on. In addition, there should be some subjective criteria. For example, team harmony is important, because many groups, even successful ones, find the group interactions unpleasant and can't wait for the project to end.

Application

Every team should have multiple goals that relate to the team's performance and the performance of its members.

Here are some examples of the different types of goals:

Objective goals
- Financial (e.g. return on investment)
- Milestones (e.g. deliver this result by 1 December)
- Performance-based (e.g. achieve specific results).

Team interaction goals
- Level of collaboration (e.g. mutual trust)
- Types of interactions (e.g. informal versus formal)
- High levels of openness and acceptance.

Learning goals
- The experience will enable the group members to learn something new.
- Members will benefit their own work or career.
- Other people in the company will be found who will benefit from a similar experience.

TOOL

Build teams around passion

We all know that if you really care about something you tend to be more effective and enjoy your work more. The principle is the same whether you are working on a new product, fixing a customer problem or tending your garden at home.

The usual procedure is to design teams based on skills, roles or the problem at hand (L1). A new lens is to design the team around interest in the topic (L2). If all team members are passionate about the task, the team is more likely to overcome the barriers to success and remain motivated to achieve the final objective.

When I was in China recently, the CEO of a large electronics business announced to the staff that every Monday from now on was passion day and they were encouraged to dress in something red. On this day, they were free to explore new projects they felt passionate about. The engineers at Google are also encouraged to spend a day a week working on projects they are passionate about. One result of this has been the launch of Google Earth.

Application

I have listed below some practical ways to build teams around passion:

- Post a team assignment on your intranet, or contact employees by email, asking them if they would like to work on the project.

- Form a team of people who share a similar interest, such as improving customer service, then look for a project to work on.

- Form a team with people you find interesting, then look for a project.

- If you have a large group, divide up into smaller groups and ask each member to nominate the part of the project they would most like to work on.

TOOL

10

Imagine the perfect team result

One way to break free of your existing mindset (L1) is to design the perfect team result first (L2). This is a counter-intuitive approach to planning. The usual approach is to carefully analyse where the team is now, where the team wants to go and then how to get there. This process usually involves a series of timelines, deliverables and milestones.

There is nothing wrong with this approach for most business-as-usual projects. However, if the team is facing a completely new challenge, or one where a breakthrough solution will be needed, it may be better to decide what the perfect result is first, then design back to the current situation.

Designing backwards means that you are not as fixed in continuing what has gone before, and the short-term barriers do not seem as big, because they are seen in the context of the perfect end result. A dance company director I interviewed indicated that this is the approach they use for their new shows. They nominate the date and location of the launch of their next show, then work back to the present. This creates a sense of urgency and a common purpose.

Application

The starting point with this approach is to initially ignore the current situation and focus only on defining the perfect result. When that has been articulated, the group can design back to the current situation.

An effective practice is to start with each group member defining what a perfect team (and individual) result might be for them. Then discuss and build a collective team understanding.

What is a perfect result?	What is stopping us achieving this result?	How can we overcome these barriers?

'A new perspective is worth at least
eighty IQ points.'

Alan Kay

(one of the pioneers of the personal computer)

5 TEN TOOLS TO HELP YOU SELL WITH MORE IMPACT

1

Understand your customer's mindset

Customers, like everyone else, have a lens through which they see you and your product or service. This lens is based on their experiences, assumptions, values and beliefs in dealing with you. If you can start to see the world as the customer does, you will be able to tailor your sales message and reinforce your customer's positive attitudes and overcome negative ones.

The most effective way to understand your customer's lens is to try to establish their mindset box. I have called this the A, B, C, E box.

The letter 'A' stands for customer assumptions. For example, most customers are interested in lower prices.

The letter 'B' is for customer beliefs. These tend to be more emotional in nature—for example, good customers will be looked after or salespeople tend to exaggerate.

The letter 'C' is for customer conventions. These are the unstated rules (or behaviours) that your company and the competition both play by. For example, it might be a convention that the customers who spend the most receive the lowest price.

The letter 'E' is for the customer's experience in dealing with your product, brand or customer service.

One real advantage of this tool is that it encourages you to adopt a customer-centric view of the world rather than a product-centric view.

Application

The aim in creating a customer's mindset box (the A, B, C, E box) is to better understand their view of you and your products. By doing so, you can design a selling approach that reinforces positive perceptions and addresses negative ones.

Customer:	Date:	
Customer's mindset box (L1)	Positive perceptions (need to affirm)	Negative perceptions (need to address)
A Their assumptions		
B Their beliefs		
C Their buying conventions		
E Their purchase experiences with you		

2

Help the customer develop a new lens

How you are seen by your customers or clients influences what products you can sell and whether your claims are believed or not. For example, when I worked in advertising I would occasionally talk to a client who thought that although the advertising campaign we had developed was good, their product was faulty or priced too high. Because I was seen as an advertising person, my advice was usually not heeded or welcomed. 'Stick to advertising' was the usual refrain. However, when I shifted careers and became a management consultant I would mention the same things to similar clients who treated my suggestions with respect.

The audit consultants from a large accounting company struggle with a similar issue. They want to be seen as business partners but the client only sees them as auditors. This limits potential opportunities for their team to work with the client.

The task therefore is to understand how you are seen by the client (that is, establish their L1, as in Tool 1) and, if their perceptions are limited, you have to help your clients form a new view of you (an L2).

Application

The first step is to articulate the opportunities and limitations of how a customer sees you now (L1).

Then you must develop a new lens (an L2) and a plan to help the client arrive at this new view.

How does my client or customer see me now (L1)?

What are the strengths of this lens?

Are there any potential limitations of this lens?

How would I like my client or customer to see me (L2)?

What are the strengths of this new lens?

Are there any potential limitations of this new lens?

What can I do to bring about this change in view?

TOOL

3

Make your selling process explicit

This tool will help you to plan your next sales call for maximum effectiveness. It asks you to make explicit the who, what, why, when, where and how of your selling process.

- Who is your key customer?
- What is your proposition?
- Why should they believe you instead of the competition?
- When can a customer use your product?
- Where can they use your product?
- How can they use your product?

These are typical questions asked by any potential customer and must be addressed by anyone in a sales role. If you develop answers to these questions in advance, then you are well prepared. This tool forces you to make your selling process explicit. By doing so, you can challenge your process and perhaps design a more effective one.

This tool should be treated as an evolving one. As you gain more experience with a particular customer you can adjust your responses accordingly. The other benefit of spelling out your selling process is that you can share your findings with the other members of your sales team to ensure that you have a uniform and consistent response.

Application

This worksheet should be completed before each new sales call and revisited every quarter.

If you are calling on a new prospect, role-play your answers to the questions with a colleague before visiting the client.

Salesperson:	Date:
1. Who is the key customer?	
2. What is your proposition?	
3. Why should they believe you?	
4. When can they use your product?	
5. Where can they use your product?	
6. How can they use your product?	

TOOL

4

Use a competitor's lens

Tool 4 is a variation on the traditional role-playing exercise in which one salesperson sells to another who is pretending to be a customer. This is a useful exercise for new salespeople to use as it will help when they have to deal with potentially difficult customers.

I have found it to be more effective if the salesperson imagines they are from the competition when they make the presentation. This 'competitor's' presentation is then compared with your own sales presentation.

Imaginary role-playing often highlights the strengths and weaknesses of your selling proposition as opposed to your competition's and gives your sales team an insight into how the competition might sell their product.

For example, an insurance sales force that I worked with were very confident of the power of their selling message. After completing this exercise, the salespeople realised that their message was almost identical to their competitor's, which opened their minds to the possibility of developing a new, differentiated selling message.

Application

A good way to use this tool is to use a worksheet to compare and contrast your selling propositions.

For example:

What is my selling proposition?	What are the strengths?	What are the weaknesses?
Premium service at a premium price	• Quality product • Strong reputation	• High price

What is my competitor's selling proposition?	What are the strengths?	What are the weaknesses?
Very good service at an affordable price	• Value for money	• Standard serve • No ability to customise

TOOL

5

Visualise your perfect sales call

One way of bringing about a new view of your current selling performance (an L2) is for you to remember and visualise a perfect sales call. It could be one you made last week or five years ago. By visualising the call, it can motivate you to repeat it time and time again.

Remembering and visualising your perfect sales call can also help you to overcome any current poor sales performance.

Sports players talk about 'the zone', where everything appears to move slowly and they seem to do everything perfectly. You, too, can experience 'the zone' in much the same way. The aim with this tool is to articulate exactly what you were thinking and feeling when you were in your sales 'zone'.

If you are having trouble remembering your perfect sales call, try to remember when you experienced a perfect call by someone else. You could have been the customer or an onlooker. What can you learn from what they were doing?

Application

Try to recapture your perfect sales presentation in all its dimensions. Then plot your latest sales call (like the example below). This will highlight your specific opportunities to improve. On a perfect sales call, you would score 100/100 on all dimensions. In the example given below, the salesperson should be concentrating on improving their ability to develop a rapport and create a win/win situation.

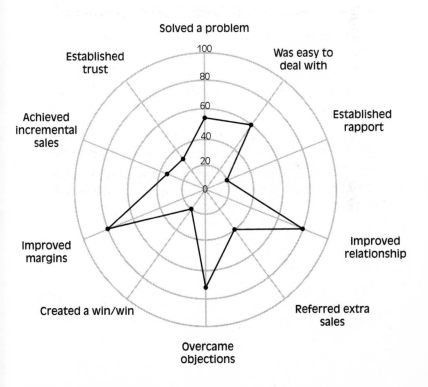

TOOL

6

Rehearse things mentally

This tool will help you to rehearse and prepare yourself before your sales call. The rehearsal occurs not in real life, but in your mind's eye. World-class athletes use the same process when they rehearse the race mentally before they compete. In this way they feel they have experienced the big event in advance. The practice helps with nerves and ensures they are fully prepared for any eventuality.

If you visualise your sales call in advance it helps you to anticipate and be prepared for any objection—you can see and feel yourself making a more successful and effective sales presentation.

Mental rehearsal is ideal for a new presentation or a difficult customer. By rehearsing what you say and how you say it, you are more relaxed and self-assured. It can also highlight any problems that the customer may have with your proposal. This allows you to try and fix these in advance or at least acknowledge them if they emerge and indicate to the customer what steps you have already taken to address them. Your client will be amazed.

Another advantage of this tool is that it can be done in a few minutes. Having run your own visualised sales presentation you are often very eager to begin the real one, because you are psychologically and emotionally prepared.

Application

This is a solo exercise. Go to a quiet place and mentally select a specific customer. Visualise that customer. What are they wearing, doing and saying as you begin your sales call? Imagine yourself as a video camera that captures every moment between you and your customer.

Visualise yourself in a selling presentation. You look and sound confident. In your mind's eye watch yourself make your sales pitch. You can tell it is going well because you can see the customer nodding. Watch yourself as you handle a number of difficult objections with ease.

Picture yourself making the sale. Your customer smiles and starts telling someone else how you have helped them.

Now rewind your video camera. What was said? What were the customer objections and how did you handle them? If you had to change tack in the presentation, what were the key turning points? What language did you use to convey a major sales message?

What did you learn, and what will you use in the actual sales call?

Revisit the worksheet in Tool 3—what can be made more effective?

TOOL

7

Design purely rational, emotional and imaginative selling propositions

A good way to break free of your existing lens (L1) is to design three different selling propositions—a rational, an emotional and an imaginative version. People buy with their heads and their hearts, something that every sports car salesperson knows. No doubt a red sports car has good resale value, but we all know it makes the driver feel younger or more powerful. Lead with the heart and support with the head.

Customers will buy from you if your product is of high quality and competitively priced (rational need), if they like and trust you (emotional need), and, more and more often, if they wish to be surprised and amazed (imaginative need).

Many salespeople tend to concentrate on the rational needs of their customers. This was very apparent to me when I was working with a large computer hardware company. All their salespeople had been trained to talk about the product in a rational way. This approach worked when selling to the finance director, but not to the customer service manager, who needed to be reassured that the company could be called upon at any time if there was a breakdown (emotional need). The salespeople also needed to develop breakthrough solutions (imaginative need). A high-performing salesperson needs to tailor their message to the different needs of their customer.

Application

Tool 7 highlights the different rational, emotional and imaginative needs, wants and expectations of customers, and how you need to address them to get the sale. The challenge is to design a purely rational, a purely emotional, and a purely imaginative selling proposition. Which one feels right for a specific customer? Can you combine the best aspects of each approach? My suggestion is that one person plays the customer and writes down their rational, emotional and imaginative needs before the role-playing begins, but does not show the other person. The seller then tries to close the sale. After each person has had a turn, their different needs are revealed and they can provide feedback on how to improve the sales call.

The customer's rational needs	The customer's emotional needs	The customer's imaginative needs
• Price • Quality • Trading terms	• Trust • Fun • Peace of mind • Fashion	• New solution • Surprise • Entertain

After completing this tool it is a good idea to revisit the Tool 3 worksheet. Is there anything you should change or update, particularly the questions dealing with what you are selling or what consumers are really buying?

TOOL 8

Isolate your customers' key problems

The traditional lens (L1) is to think in terms of your product features and benefits. A different lens (L2) is to think in terms of the key problems your customers face, and how you could solve these for them. If you can solve a customer problem, then your customer will appreciate it and reward you with more business.

For example, consider the customer problem, 'What are we going to do on Saturday night?' The solution? A pizza and DVD deal.

Notice how the solution involved another business. It is sometimes the case that you cannot do everything yourself. These situations often create a win/win situation—the customer obtains a better deal and both businesses gain incremental revenue. The important point is that your focus is on solving the customer's problem. In fact, your role in sales or account management is to be the customer problem/solution champion.

The other advantage of this tool is that it provides you with a way to think in terms of customers' problems—an 'outside in' view—rather than the more traditional 'inside out' view.

Application

This worksheet encourages you to think of the customer's problem first, then how to solve it. Select a key customer's problem, then develop a business-as-usual, different and radical way of solving it (see Chapter 1, Tool 5). Then select the best option—it could be a combination of the three solutions.

Customer:	Date:

The problem:

A business-as-usual solution:

A different solution:

A radical solution:

TOOL 9

Establish mutually agreed objectives and criteria for success

When you are presenting a new idea to a client, the usual lens (L1) is to make your pitch and then wait for the evaluation.

One way to change this situation is to try to establish the criteria—how your proposal will be judged—with the client before you start your pitch. This helps you to sell your message, because you can be evaluated against the previously agreed criteria.

Try to remember a successful sales presentation you have made. I bet part of the reason for your success was that you understood very clearly what the client was looking for. If you are presenting a new idea that appeals to the head and the heart, an effective approach is to try to develop rational, emotional and imaginative criteria (see Tool 7) to determine the success of the ideas that you present.

This is one of the favourite ploys of the advertising executive: they remind everyone of the communication brief objectives just prior to presenting the new advertisement.

Application

Remember your last sales call? What, in your opinion, were the rational, emotional and imaginative criteria the client was using to judge your proposal? How could you change your next proposal to completely satisfy these criteria?

| Customer: | | Date: |

	What is my rating (out of 10)?	How could I improve?
Rational criteria: Did I answer the brief?		
Emotional criteria: Did they like me?		
Imaginative criteria: Was my proposal different to my competitor's?		

TOOL

10

Use an unsuccessful sales call as an opportunity to learn

If there is one thing I have learned from running my own business, it is that you have to learn to live with rejection. If a proposal has been rejected, perhaps it didn't come at the right time or the style of the presentation might not have been appropriate for the audience. With some modifications, it may receive a more sympathetic hearing at a later date. This is why it is important to shift your lens from viewing rejection as a defeat (L1) to an opportunity to learn and do better next time (L2).

Try to figure out exactly why your proposal was rejected. Was it the core selling message or the way it was expressed? By varying the execution slightly, the proposition might be accepted next time. When I run my workshops I often invite attendees to talk about a time in their life when they tried something new, and to discuss where they came up short, what they learned and what the results were. They soon realise that trying and failing is a normal part of life and is often followed by periods of intense personal and business growth.

Remember that it is the proposition that is being rejected, not you as a person. Although it can be disheartening, rejection can make us stronger and more determined. Every rejection should be treated as another opportunity to learn, or as Thomas Edison remarked, 'We now know what doesn't work; let's find out what does.'

Application

An effective way of dealing with rejection is to gather other sales team members together and start talking about it. Sometimes you can feel as though you are the only person that has had an unsuccessful sales call, but everybody has failures from time to time.

Ask the most successful salespeople how they cope with a sales rejection. It is natural to feel disappointed, but you should always be asking yourself, 'What can I learn from this so that I can improve my chances next time?'

What can I learn from my last unsuccessful sales call?	What can I change that will improve my chances next time?

'It's easy to come up with new ideas;
the hard part is letting go of what
worked for you two years ago, but will
soon be out of date.'

Roger Von Oech, *A Whack on the Side of the Head*

6 TEN TOOLS TO DELIVER BREAKTHROUGH LEADERSHIP RESULTS

Study growth businesses systematically

Most managers that I work with keep a very close eye on their competition, industry shifts and consumer trends. Their motive is to grow the business and stay ahead of the competition.

Yet they rarely study other growth brands or businesses in a systematic way. This new lens (L2) can often provide a rich source of new growth ideas that could be utilised by your business. For example, McDonald's, after years of growing mainly through opening new sites, is now building incremental revenue through a deliberate repositioning around health. Is this strategy something that you could borrow, learn or adapt?

What growth businesses should you keep an eye on now and which ones should you consider in the future?

Application

Draw up a list of growth businesses outside your industry. There is no right or wrong list—the more unrelated the businesses the better.

Once you have this list, commit to studying one of these brands every month. You could allocate this task to an individual, a small team or, for example, someone from your advertising agency. Better still, invite a leader from the brand you are studying to make a presentation to your management team about what they are doing to grow their business.

The aim is to spend a few hours studying and talking about what the growth business is doing and what you could borrow, learn or adapt.

For example:

What are some examples of growth businesses?	What can I take from them to apply to my business?
Proctor & Gamble	Their use of suppliers and partners to help them co-create new ideas and business opportunities.

TOOL

2

Tell your leadership story

One very powerful way of motivating people is through story-telling.[1] Stories tend to be better at engaging people's heads and hearts than facts alone. Stories can provide a new lens (or L2) through which people can see their current situation, a future direction or a reason to change.

At 3M, for example, their leaders are continually retelling the Art Fry story (the inventor of the Post-it note). This story highlights many of the beliefs about innovation at 3M. It is a story of one person's passion and perseverance in spite of numerous obstacles.

A leader can direct formally through organisation power and position, or they can inspire through example and by their own stories. As a leader, what is your most inspiring leadership story? Once you have articulated your leadership story, try to use it in most of your important presentations, particularly with new staff.

Application

Listed below are two ways to apply this concept.

1. Study your favourite non-business leader

Who is your favourite leader in or outside business? Reflect on their leadership story. For example, Mahatma Gandhi's story is one of forgiveness and perseverance in spite of long years of captivity. He treated even his harshest critics with respect and dignity. As a leader, ask yourself what you could learn from his story.

2. Recall your best leadership moment

Another effective tool is to recall some of your own best leadership moments. It could be at work or on the sporting field. Try to remember the exact feeling of leading a team to achieve a goal or victory. What is the story of this achievement? What could you learn from this story?

3

Study leaders outside business

Who do you really admire in business? I have asked this question literally hundreds of times in my workshops and the list is very thin. Bill Gates, Steve Jobs and Anita Roddick are sometimes mentioned, but not often with a great deal of passion.

Why is this so? My experience is that many profit leaders' lenses are often based on an outdated power, command and control way of thinking.[2] In a world built on collaboration, flexibility, speed and imagination, a new lens is needed.

Based on my research into creativity in organisations, I believe that a new leadership approach can be found by looking at leadership as practised in cultural and non-profit settings. Here the leader has to inspire by word and deed. They face constant challenges with limited resources. This requires both emotional and creative intelligence.

Let's consider someone like Jamie Oliver, for example. What is it about his leadership style that demands respect? Perhaps it is his infectious enthusiasm, his passion or his knowledge. Probably it is his authenticity and tremendous sense of self that we most admire. Is this something that we can all learn from?

Application

Nominate five leaders you admire outside business: for example, Oprah Winfrey.

The leaders do not have to be famous—they could be a local church leader or school principal. Outline the aspects of their leadership style that you admire.

Ask each team member to choose one of their selection and draw out what it is about their leadership style they admire and can learn.

What leaders do I admire?	What can I borrow, learn or adapt from their leadership styles?

TOOL

4

Choose a world-class business to benchmark against

Many business leaders are very keen on benchmarking. They place great store on the results of their benchmarking and where their business stands relative to the competition.

But when you ask them which businesses or brands they benchmark against and why, they go strangely quiet. I recently completed an assignment with a major bank—the leaders were satisfied when they compared their customer service levels with other banks. I suggested that perhaps they were not necessarily comparing themselves with the best markers, and that they could gain a real breakthrough by comparing their service with, for example, a five-star hotel. By comparing your business with other similar businesses, you perpetuate your current view of the world (L1). In other words, you tend to see evidence that supports your long-held beliefs or assumptions. If, on the other hand, you use a different lens (L2) by comparing your business with the best in the world on a specific dimension (e.g. Apple and product design) your comfortable world is shaken and new growth opportunities or areas of improvement become apparent.

Benchmarking can be a very effective tool if it challenges, not reinforces, your existing lens.

Application

Write down five key functions or activities that you are responsible for. Then select a business that is a world-class exponent of this activity.

What can you learn from this business?

For example:

What is my key function or activity?	What is the world-class benchmark?	What can I learn, borrow or adapt?
Manufacturing	Toyota	Involving the employees in the quality control and design of a better system

5

TOOL

Drive innovative behaviour

Leaders acknowledge that creating internal growth requires innovation. Attempts are often made to change employees' attitudes through various vision, mission and values statements.

These are important, but innovation also requires a change in behaviour. To illustrate this concept, think about trying to lose weight. You can have all the right intentions and know which foods to avoid, but unless you actually start going for walks and eating salad instead of pie, you won't lose weight.

Innovation requires a similar change in behaviour. The leaders of Deloitte, a major accounting firm, insist that every manager does something innovative with a client every 20 days and then comes back and presents what happened.

Innovation needs more than slogans and being part of a firm's value statements. While these are important, innovative behaviour must be experienced.

Application

I have listed below some examples of innovative behaviour that you might find useful as a leader:

- Set up an innovation fund. This could be sourced (for example) by taking 5 per cent of your current budget and allocating it to developing new growth projects.

- Ask for a business-as-usual, different and radical proposal for all new problems (see Chapter 1, Tool 5).

- Allow a formal 'gut feel' time in every meeting, particularly after a decision has been reached. Ask everyone what their gut feelings are about the decision.

- Post a different problem every day on the intranet and ask employees to help resolve it.

- Always be testing three new ideas at any point in time.

- Take at least one calculated risk every week.

TOOL

6

Work back from the opportunity

The traditional way to build a new revenue growth stream is to leverage one of your existing strengths. For example, Nudie juices have now entered the ice cream market, hoping to capitalise on their brand loyalty.

Sometimes a more productive lens (L2) is to identify the growth opportunity first, then build a bridge back to the business. In a sense, the leader must practise right-to-left thinking rather than the usual left-to-right approach.

I once worked with the leaders of a large health insurance business that had identified healthy people as a potential untapped market. They had no trouble identifying the opportunity, but realised they knew little about the insurance needs and expectations of healthy people. This led to the commissioning of a large-scale research study to better understand this segment's needs.

Leaders have discovered that working back from the opportunity means that anything is possible and they do not get 'bogged down' in the many small problems that often emerge at the start of any new project.

Application

Working back from the opportunity requires you to use right-to-left thinking. This will enable you to better see the possible connection back to your business.

The steps you need to undertake to bring about this shift in thinking are outlined below:

1. Identify the opportunity—for example, an aging population, or people who speak English as a second language.

2. Design the perfect proposition to leverage the opportunity.

3. Compare and contrast the perfect proposition with your current offering, and outline the gaps or deficiencies.

4. Start work today on closing the gaps as you work towards building a bridge between the opportunity and your business.

TOOL

7

Re-imagine your business

Perhaps the ultimate leadership challenge is to build a sustainable, adaptable business. This may require an occasional re-imagining of the type of business you are in.

By defining your business too narrowly, you are closing your mind to new growth opportunities. For example, Starbucks defined themselves as sellers of coffee, but this lens (L1) limited the leaders to only considering coffee-related opportunities. Now the leaders have re-imagined their business as becoming the third place for consumers (after home and work) to spend time. This has led to the introduction of other potential growth areas, such as selling music at their outlets. One of their new aims is to become one of the biggest music retailers in the world.

A re-imagining of your business can only be achieved if you change the way you look at doing business. For example, according to the 9/11 commission report, one of the major problems of the US government was a 'failure of imagination'. The officials simply could not imagine there would ever be an attack on their own shores on the scale of the 9/11 attack on the twin towers.

Using this tool will allow you to break free from a limited perspective.

Application

A good starting point for re-imagining your business is to consider your current business definition, then create a number of different definitions. The emphasis is on using a different lens. After you have created a number of different lenses, ask yourself who your new competitors are. If your competitors are similar, then you may have to use a wider lens.

Let's imagine you are the leader of an advertising agency, and you want to create new growth opportunities by re-imagining your business definition:

Lens in use	Competitors
Current lens: 'We are in the advertising business'	Other advertising agencies
New lens: 'We are in the communication business'	Other advertising agencies, PR companies, strategy consultants
New lens: 'We are in the ideas business'	Other advertising agencies, PR companies, strategy consultants, authors, academics, Disney, Ideo

Thrive on an open mind policy

Many leaders profess to having an open door policy. By this they presumably mean that they wish to encourage their team to openly and regularly discuss issues that impact on their performance at work.

However, it has been my experience that the employees feel that although the door of the leader's office is open, the leader's mind is not. This sends mixed messages to the employees. In effect, what the leader is saying is that their door is only open to ideas they agree with.

I recently dealt with the marketing director of a fast food brand whose sales were in decline. I mentioned that the brand managers had many fresh and potentially breakthrough ideas. He indicated that these managers could do anything they wanted as long as it was consistent with the annual marketing plan. The fact that the plan was not working seemed to have eluded the marketing director.

An open mind means you actively encourage ideas from people who have a different lens on the world.

Application

Leaders have found that the LIFT framework, outlined below, is helpful in encouraging a greater exploration of potential new ideas.

Listen:

Actively listen to the idea. One good way is to repeat the idea to the idea creator to ensure that you have understood it fully.

Improve:

When you understand the idea, discuss ways the idea could be improved or enhanced with the idea's creator. Try not to evaluate the idea at this stage. Highlight what you like about the idea and discuss how it could become even stronger.

Feedback:

Provide direct, honest and constructive feedback. Decide together if the new idea is worth testing.

Test:

Suggest ways to test the idea quickly, easily and cheaply.

TOOL 9

Change your lens, then the marketplace

Classic business and marketing theory suggests that you must adopt an external or customer's orientation to see new growth opportunities or unsatisfied consumer needs (L1).

My experience is that you only need to examine the marketplace after you have explored your individual and collective lenses, because it is often your own lens, rather than the market's, that will limit your opportunities. Your own self-beliefs and assumptions often restrict your view of a market.

For example, I once worked with the leadership team of a fire extinguisher business. They described their business as one that was in decline due to competition from China. Profit margins were shrinking and they were very pessimistic. When I asked the leaders what their perspective of their business was (their L1), they replied that fire extinguishers were a grudge purchase mandated by law. I encouraged them to play around with a different lens (L2) and they came up with 'fire extinguishers can be both necessary and beautiful'. With this new perspective, they re-imagined their target market as every household in the country (a much larger potential audience) and developed a new glow-in-the-dark version. Suddenly their business was filled with new growth opportunities.

Application

When I conduct workshops with leaders, I often ask them a series of questions in an attempt to challenge their existing lens. By doing so, they realise that their own lens might control the key to further growth opportunities.

The questions I ask are set out below:

1. What is stopping Virgin entering your category or industry? After all, this brand has a major presence in such diverse industries as airlines, banking and soft-drinks.

2. If you were the Virgin management team, how would you enter your industry?

3. As a leadership team, what should you be doing right now to ensure that Virgin cannot consider such a move?

TOOL

10

Have a revenue growth goal

This tool is a provocative and challenging one. My suggestion is that every leader or manager, regardless of title, function or responsibility, should have a revenue growth goal.

The advantage of this approach is that it challenges every leader to think of new and different ways to create new growth opportunities. Imagine the impact on your balance sheet if you had everyone thinking of revenue growth, not just those in marketing and sales. The other benefit is that leaders will be more receptive to new ideas if they know they have to think about revenue and not just about cost-cutting.

I introduced this new challenge (P2) to the CEO of a major hotel and his leadership team. After the usual disquiet among the leadership team, the manager of hotel security suggested that his security was not active for 40 per cent of their time. He believed he could sell this 'down time' to other hotels and restaurants near their location, and for the first time break even on their security services.

Sometimes to create disruptive ideas and behaviour you have to set a disruptive challenge.

Application

Every manager, regardless of role, should at least attempt to have a revenue growth goal, even if it is to break even. Use the worksheet below to develop a new goal and an approach that indicates how you can deliver it. What resources might you need to deliver some incremental revenue? What might be stopping you?

For example:

What is my potential revenue growth goal?	How can I reach my goal?
To increase customer average spend from $6 to $8 (actual goal of a well-known fast food outlet)	Introduce a new lunchtime menu

CONCLUSION

This book has been written with the time-poor manager in mind. My aim is to help anyone in business to become a more innovative thinker and produce better results.

My belief is that we can all perform at a higher level. Achieving this means learning a new way of thinking that will compliment your existing approach. This new thinking model is built on the assumption that if you want a different and more original set of ideas you must either:

- Change the way you look at a problem (opportunity or issue), and/or
- Change the nature of the problem.

Otherwise you are doomed to become stuck in your thinking. In this book I have provided you with a new set of tools that will enable you to see a problem with fresh eyes and/or redefine the problem. It will free you up to create a range of breakthrough ideas and solutions.

The tools are effective and practical but require some practice and perseverance. They can be easily learned and applied to most situations you will face at work and in life generally. Most importantly, they work. Participants in my workshops feel they can out-think their competition and get ahead. So can you.

THE IDEA GENERATOR

I believe that successful businesses in the future will rely more and more on people. In particular, those people who can design new and original solutions to problems or create new growth opportunities. The tools in *The Idea Generator* will enable you to unlock your own creative thinking potential and deliver real results almost immediately. Your imagined future is in your hands.

NOTES

Introduction

1. This is similar to the terminology 'a current view of a situation to a better view of a situation' proposed by M. Hewitt-Gleeson, *Software for the Brain 2*, Wrightbooks: North Brighton, Victoria, 1991. I have also been influenced by L. Bolman, *Reframing Organizations: Artistry, choice and leadership*, Jossey-Bass Publishers: San Francisco, 1991.

2. For a very good description of mindsets see J.A. Barker, *Paradigms: Understand the future in business and in life*, William Morrow & Co.: New York, 1992.

3. Edward de Bono calls these 'patterns'. See E. de Bono, *The Mechanism of Mind*, Penguin: London, 1969.

4. J. Welch, *Jack*, Warner Books Inc.: New York, 2001, p. 202.

5. E.F. Vencat, 'Forces of nature', *Newsweek*, 14 August 2006, p. 41.

Chapter 2

1. Adapted from R. Fritz, *Creating*, Butterworth-Heinemann: Oxford, 1991.

2. A. Koestler, *The Act of Creation*, Penguin: London, 1964.

Chapter 3

1. My work has been influenced by the cognitive approaches developed by Howard Gardner, *Frames of Mind: The theory of multiple intelligence*, HarperCollins: New York, 1993, *Creating Minds: An anatomy of creativity*, HarperCollins: New York, 1993, and *Changing Minds: The art and science of changing our own and other people's minds*, Harvard Business School Press: Boston, 2004.

2. For a review of the importance placed on a sports person's mental approaches see D. Hemery, *Sporting Excellence: What makes a champion?*, HarperCollins: London, 1991. See also W.T. Gallwey, *The Inner Game of Work*, Texere: London, 2002, for a very good discussion of how sporting principles have been applied to work situations.

3. 'The Seeds of Apple Innovation', *Business Week Online*, 12 October 2004.

Chapter 4

1. For a wonderful discussion on what makes a great group, see W. Bennis, *Organizing Genius: The secrets of creative colloboration*, Addison-Wesley: Reading, MA, 1997.

2. My proposition of different thinking styles has been influenced by A.J. Rowe, *Creative Intelligence*, Prentice Hall: NJ, 2004, and R.J. Sternberg, *Thinking Styles*, Cambridge University Press: Cambridge, 1997. I have also been influenced by the work of D. Goleman, *Emotional Intelligence: Why it can matter more than I.Q.*, Bloomsbury: London, 1996.

3. For the power of *and* versus *or* thinking, see J.C. Collins and J.I. Porras, *Built to Last: Successful habits of visionary companies*, Random House: Sydney, 1994.

NOTES

Chapter 6

1. See also H. Gardner and E. Laskin, *Leading Minds: An anatomy of leadership*, HarperCollins: New York, 1996.
2. A. Sinclair, *Doing Leadership Differently: Gender, power and sexuality in a changing business culture*, Melbourne University Press: Melbourne, 1998.

FURTHER READING

Buzan, T., *Make the Most of Your Mind*, Simon & Schuster: New York, 1988.

Couger, J.D., *Creative Problem Solving and Opportunity Finding*, Boyd & Fraser: Danvers, MA, 1995.

Csikszentmihali, M., *Creativity: Flow and the psychology of discovery and invention*, Harper Perennial: New York, 1996.

de Bono, E., *Serious Creativity: Using the power of lateral thinking to create new ideas*, HarperCollins: London, 1992.

Fritz, R., *Creating*, Butterworth-Heinemann: Oxford, UK, 1991.

Garner, H., *Creating Minds: An anatomy of creativity*, HarperCollins: New York, 1993.

Goleman, D., *Emotional Intelligence: Why this can matter more than I.Q.*, Bloomsbury Publishing: London, 1996.

Grudin, R., *The Grace of Great Things: Creativity and innovation*, Houghton Mifflin Company: Boston, MA, 1990.

Hamel, G., 'Strategy as revolution', *Harvard Business Review*, July–August, pp. 69–82, 1996.

Hewitt-Gleeson, M., *Software for the Brain 2*, Wrightbooks: North Brighton, Victoria, 1991.

Kao, J., *Jamming: The art and discipline of business creativity*, HarperCollins: New York, 1996.

Koestler, A., *The Act of Creation*, Penguin: London, 1964.

FURTHER READING

Leonard, D. and Swap, W., *When Sparks Fly: Igniting creativity in groups*, Harvard Businss School Press: Boston, MA, 1999.

Nachmanovitch, S., *Free Play: The power of improvisation in life and the art*, G.P. Putnam's Songs: New York, 1990.

NOTES

NOTES

NOTES